Better Vocals Witl

Rockschool

A Rockschool Publication
www.rockschool.co.uk

Welcome To Level 1 *Male Vocals*

Welcome to the Rockschool Level 1 candidate pack for Male Vocals. This pack includes all the prepared elements needed by a candidate to take grades 1, 2 and 3. In the book you will find exam scores for the performance pieces consisting of a vocal line and chord boxes.

The CDs have backing tracks for the technical exercises; five of the songs in each grade have two backing tracks in different keys. Examples of all the other tests contained in the exam can be found in the *Companion Guide* accompanying this series.

If you have any queries about this or any other Rockschool exam, please call us on **0845 460 4747** or email us at office@rockschool.co.uk. Visit our website http://www.rockschool.co.uk. Good luck!

Grade 1

At this grade there will be an emphasis on notes, rhythm and intonation. Pieces will generally be within a limited range and only require a basic control of tone. Pieces will be of a length appropriate for the grade and there will be no requirement for vocal improvisation. The use of a microphone is not mandatory but candidates may use one if they feel it will enhance their performance.

Grade 2

At this grade there will be an emphasis on basic style awareness in the use of tone and solid voice. There may be limited use of head voice. Pieces will be of slightly longer duration with an extended range and the use of intervallic leaps.

Grade 3

At this grade there will be an increasing level of stylistic awareness with employment of suitable technique to a basic level. There will be use of solid voice and a limited requirement for head voice. Pieces will be of a suitable length to demonstrate appropriate technique and concentration with an extended range and occasional use of wide intervals.

How To Use The CDs

The Level 1 book contains two CDs. On these you will find the backing tracks to the exercises and the songs. Candidates should prepare the exercises and the songs using these CDs to perform with in the exam.

For the scales and intervals in grades 1, 2 and 3, the first backing track is in the key of A. You will find alternative keys for the scales at the end of the CD in all keys between B♭ and E around middle C. For the intervals, test 1, there are alternative notes from B♭ to B, and for test 2, there are alternative fifths from B♭ to B. Any of these keys can be used in the exam.

Important Information For Candidates

Candidates may use this syllabus to enter for either a *grade exam* or a *performance certificate* at grades 1, 2 or 3. If you are entering for a *grade exam*, you will need to prepare the following elements. You will perform them in the exam in the order in which they are shown below. Full syllabus requirements can be found in the *Rockschool Vocal Syllabus Guide* which can be downloaded from www.rockschool.co.uk.

Technical exercises (15 marks). You will find four sets of exercises printed for each grade: a rhythm test, a scale test, an interval test and a Phrasing & Dynamics test.

General Musicianship Questions (5 marks). You will be asked four questions immediately after the Phrasing & Dynamics test. These questions will focus on aspects of music notation. One final question will be asked at the end of the exam.

- **Grade 1**. 4 questions on dynamic markings and meanings, note values and time signature. 1 question on meaning of lyrics in 1 song.
- **Grade 2**. 4 questions on the above and pitch names, cresc/decresc, rest values. 1 question on expression and performance of 1 song.
- **Grade 3**. 4 questions on the above and recognition of intervals of 2nd and 3rd between two adjacent notes (candidates will not be required to state major or minor), staccato marks, slurs, pitch names within a bar (ie bar 5, 3rd beat, what is the pitch name of that note?) 1 question on expression and performance of 1 song.

Aural Tests (10 marks). There are two aural tests in each grade. Examples are printed in the Companion Guide. The requirements for each grade are as follows:

- **Grade 1**. You will be given a set of three rhythmic examples that are two bars long each. The examiner will play one of the examples on CD and you will be asked to identify the correct answer from the printed examples. You will then be asked to clap back the rhythm and to continue for two further bars in a simple/repetitive manner.
- **Grade 2**. As for Grade 1 but with more complex rhythmic values.
- **Grade 3**. As for Grade 1 but there will be a two bar melody in the same rhythm. You will be asked to sing back the melody and continue to improvise for a further two bars, returning to the tonic. The second test is a two bar chord sequence repeated over eight bars. The candidate will hear the sequence through once and will be required to improvise a major line on the repeat, paying attention to rhythmic repetition and shape. Please refer to the *Syllabus Guide* for specifications. **This test is continuous**.

Three performance pieces (60 marks). You are not limited solely to the songs printed in this book, or the companion Level 1 volume. You may perform **either** three songs from this book (including one or more from the supplementary list printed for each grade), or you may bring in **one** song not included in these lists to perform in the exam. This may be a hit from the chart or a song of your own composing. Please ensure, though, that you have the appropriate backing track. Please turn to the Guru's Guide on page 55 for the list of supplementary material.

Unaccompanied Piece (10 Marks). In addition, you will be asked to perform either a part of one of the pieces you have performed, or a different song, unaccompanied. You will be asked to sing this after you have performed the second accompanied song you have chosen. Please refer to the *Syllabus Guide* for the variation and improvisation requirements.

If you are entering a *performance certificate*, you will perform **five** songs, of which up to **two** may be from repertoire not included in this book or the companion Level 1 volume.

The Level 1 *Male Vocals* book is a companion to the Level 1 *Female Vocals* book. Candidates are welcome to perform repertoire contained in either book in the exam of equivalent difficulty.

Grade 1 *Technical Exercises*

In this section, the examiner will ask you to perform the four exercises printed below. You do not need to memorise the exercises (and you may use the book in the exam) but the examiner will be looking for the speed and confidence of your response. The examiner will also give you credit for the level of your musicality.

Exercise 1: Rhythm

Disc 1 Track 1

You will be asked to perform the exercise below as written to a backing track accompaniment in the exam. A short sound check will be given.

Exercise 2: Scales

Disc 1 Track 2

You will be asked to perform a major scale in the following rhythms to a backing track accompaniment in the exam. You will be allowed to choose your own starting note between **A-E** which will be played to you before you begin. You will be asked a selection by the examiner and you will perform the exercise *legato* to a sound of your own choosing.

Exercise 3: Intervals

This exercise has two parts - (A) You will be asked to pitch a major third above the notes **I**, **IV** and **V** of the chosen key in the above scale. The examiner will play the note for four beats on a CD and you will be asked to hold the note for four beats.

Disc 1 Track 3

(B) You will be asked to pitch the root note of a perfect fifth chosen from the same notes **I**, **IV** and **V**. The examiner will play the interval for four beats on a CD and you will be asked to hold the note for four beats.

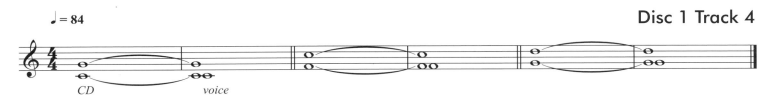

Disc 1 Track 4

Exercise 4: Phrasing & Dynamics

Disc 1 Track 5

You will be asked to prepare the following exercise. The examiner will play the backing on CD and you will be asked to sing the exercise, paying attention to the written phrasing and dynamics. You may perform the exercise using any sound that you consider appropriate.

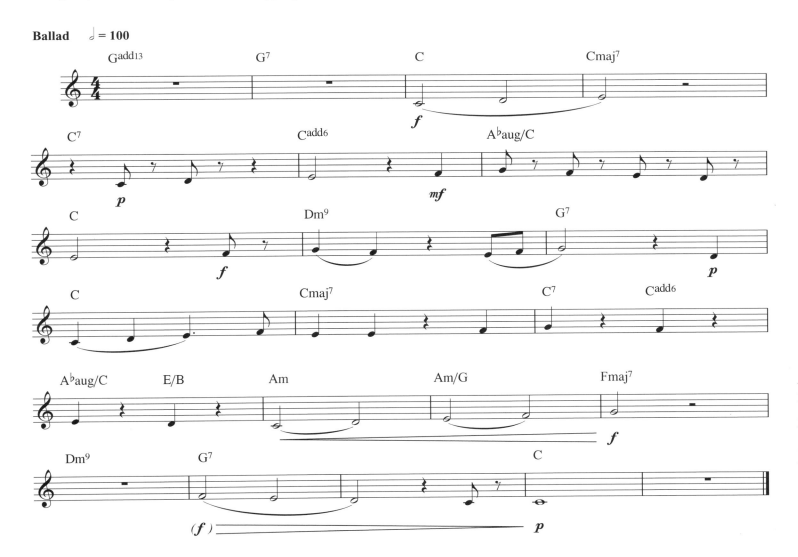

She Loves You

Words & Music by John Lennon & Paul McCartney

She loves you, yeah, yeah, yeah. She loves you, yeah,

(* alternative key)

yeah, yeah. She loves you, yeah, yeah, yeah, yeah. 1. You

Verse

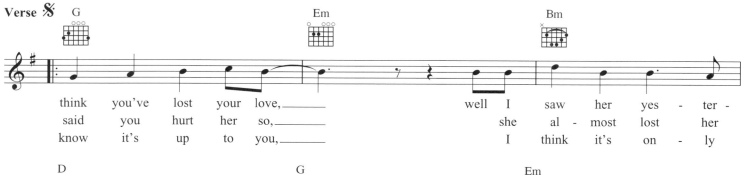

think you've lost your love, well I saw her yes-ter-
said you hurt her so, she al-most lost her
know it's up to you, I think it's on-ly

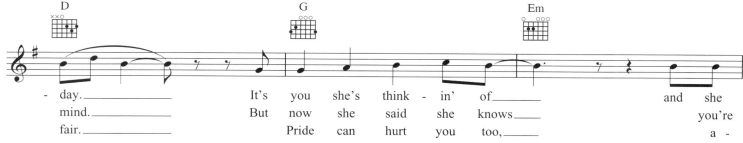

-day. It's you she's think-in' of and she
mind. But now she said she knows you're
fair. Pride can hurt you too, a-

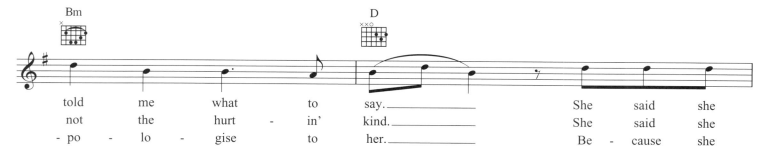

told me what to say. She said she
not the hurt-in' kind. She said she
-po-lo-gise to her. Be-cause she

loves you and you know that can't be bad, yes she

Vocals Level 1 - Male

Teenage Kicks

Words & Music by John O'Neill

Intro

Verse

1, 3. Are teen-age dreams so hard to beat___ ev-'ry time she walks___ ___ down the street?___ An-oth-er girl in the neigh-bour-hood,___ wish she was mine, she looks so good.___ I wan-na hold her, wan-na hold her tight,___ get teen-age kicks right through the night.___

Verse

2, 4. I'm gon-na call her on the te-le-phone,___ have her ov-er 'cause I'm all a-lone.___ I need ex-cite-ment, oh I need it bad,___

Rave On

Words & Music by Sunny West,
Bill Tilghman & Norman Petty

1. A - w - e - e - e - ell the lit - tle things___ you___ say and do___
(* alternative key) way you dance___ and___ hold me tight,___ the

make me want___ to___ be with you - ou - ou, rave on, it's a
way you kiss___ and___ say good - ni - igh - ight,

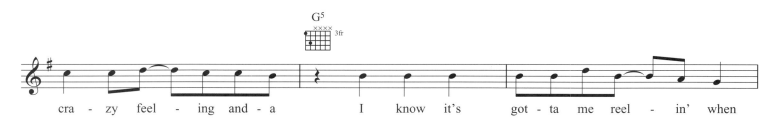

cra - zy feel - ing and - a I know it's got - ta me reel - in' when

you say,___ "I love you,"_____ rave on.

1.

2. The

2.

Oh well, rave on,_____ it's a

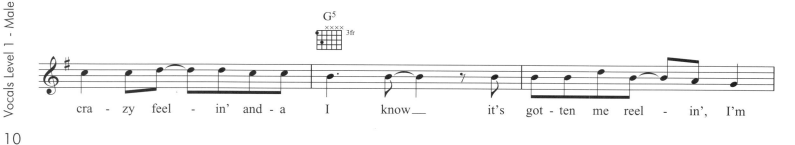

cra - zy feel - in' and - a I know___ it's got - ten me reel - in', I'm

Vocals Level 1 - Male

Fields Of Gold

Words & Music by Sting

© Copyright 1992 Magnetic Publishing Limited/
EMI Music Publishing Limited.
All Rights Reserved. International Copyright Secured.

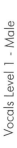

Swear It Again

Words & Music by
Steve Mac & Wayne Hector

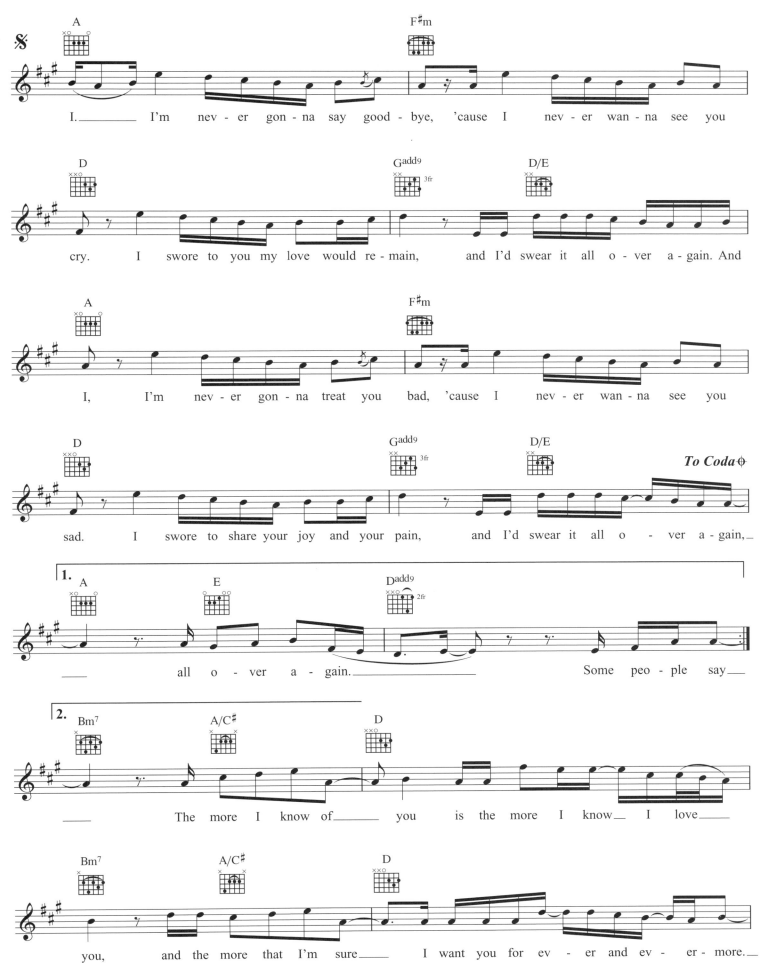

Verse 2:

Some people say that everything has got its place and time
Even the day must give way to the night
But I'm not buying.
'Cause in your eyes, I see a love that burns eternally
And if you see how beautiful you are to me
You'll know I'm not lying.
Sure, there'll be times we wanna say goodbye
But even if we tried
There are some things in this life won't be denied
Won't be denied.

I'm never gonna say goodbye *etc.*

Disco 2000

Words by Jarvis Cocker
Music by Pulp

1. Well we were

(* alternative key)

Verse

born with-in an hour of each oth-er, our moth-ers

(verse 2 see block lyrics)

said we could be sis-ter and broth-er, your name is De-bo-rah, De-bo-rah,___

___ it nev-er suit-ed ya. And they

said that when we grew up___ we'd get mar-ried and nev-er split up,___

on 𝄋 Do it!

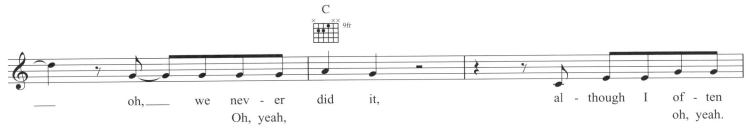

___ oh,___ we nev-er did it, al-though I of-ten
Oh, yeah, oh, yeah.

Vocals Level 1 - Male

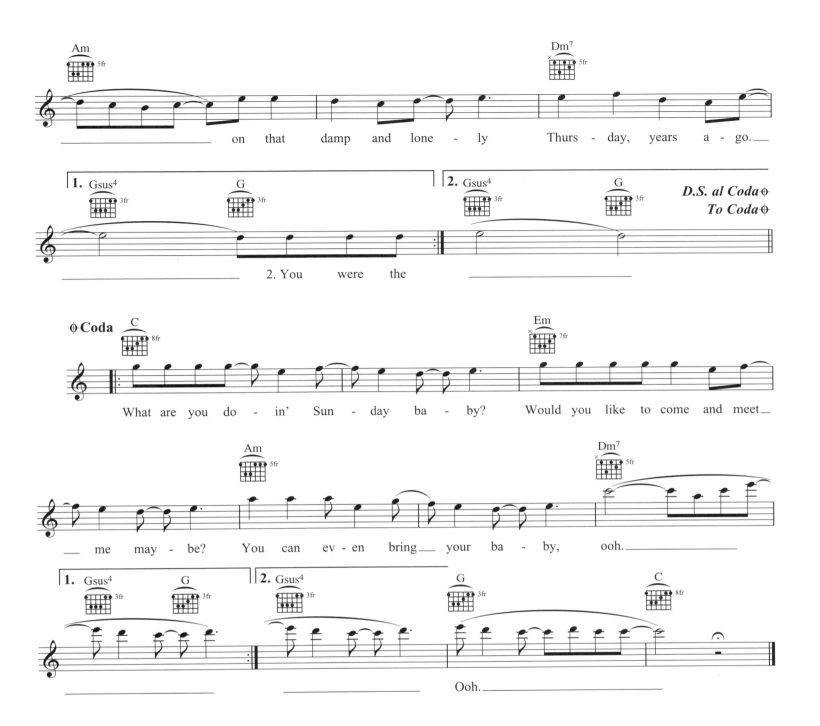

Verse 2:

You were the first girl at school to get breasts
Martyn said that yours were the best
The boys all loved you but I was a mess
I had to watch them try and get you undressed.
We were friends, that was as far as it went
I used to walk you home sometimes but it meant
Oh, it meant nothing to you
'Cause you were so popular.

Grade 2 *Technical Exercises*

In this section, the examiner will ask you to perform the four exercises printed below. You do not need to memorise the exercises (and you may use the book in the exam) but the examiner will be looking for the speed and confidence of your response. The examiner will also give you credit for the level of your musicality.

Exercise 1: Rhythm

Disc 1 Track 17

You will be asked to perform the exercise below as written to a backing track accompaniment in the exam. A short sound check will be given.

Exercise 2: Scales

Disc 1 Track 18

You will be asked to perform a major, natural and harmonic minor scale in the following rhythms to a backing track accompaniment in the exam. You will be allowed to choose your own starting note between **A-E** which will be played to you before you begin. You will be asked a selection by the examiner and you will perform the exercise *legato* to a sound of your own choosing.

Major

Natural Minor

Harmonic Minor

Exercise 3: Intervals

This exercise has two parts. (A) You will be asked to pitch a major or minor third or perfect fifth above notes **I**, **IV** and **V** of the chosen key in the above scale. The examiner will play the note for four beats on a CD and you will be asked to hold the note for four beats.

Disc 1 Track 19

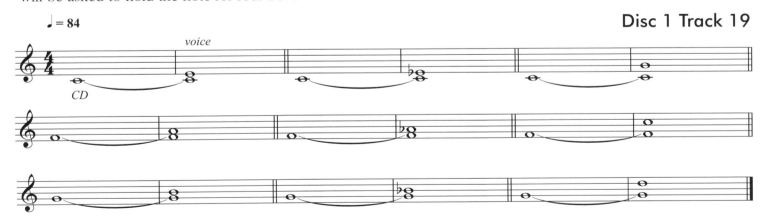

(B) You will be asked to pitch the root note of a perfect fifth chosen from the same notes. The examiner will play the interval for four beats on a CD and you will be asked to hold the note for four beats.

Disc 1 Track 20

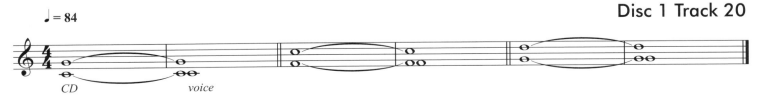

Exercise 4: Phrasing & Dynamics

You will be asked to prepare the following exercise. The examiner will play the backing on CD and you will be asked to sing the exercise, paying attention to the written phrasing and dynamics. You may perform the exercise using any sound that you consider appropriate.

When You Say Nothing At All

Words & Music by Don Schlitz & Paul Overstreet

Disc 1 Track 22/23

Vocals Level 1 - Male

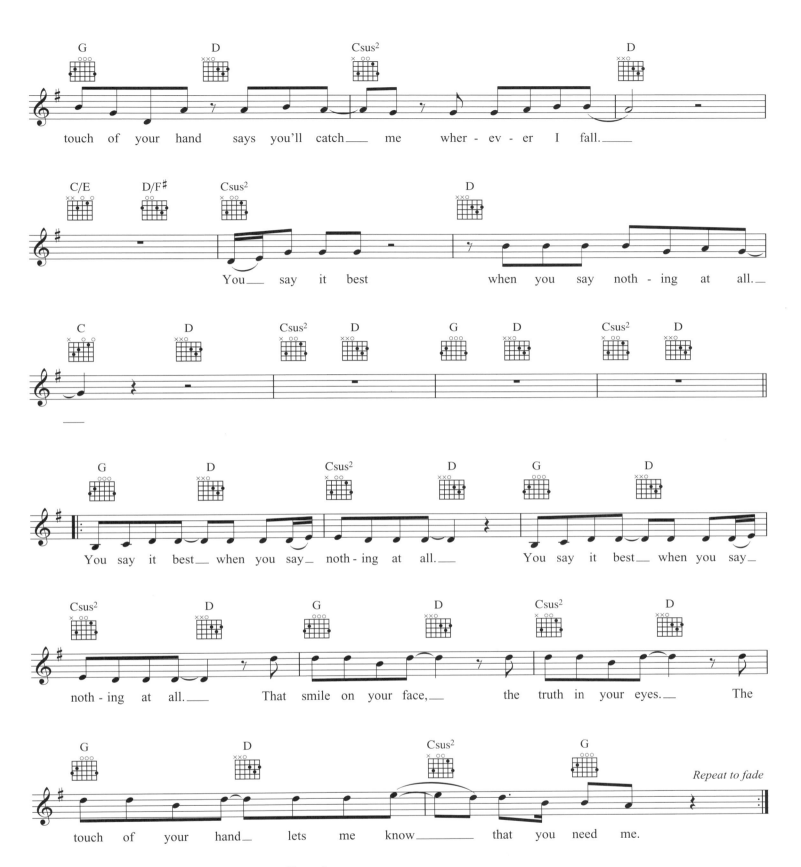

Verse 2:

All day long I can hear people talking out loud
But when you hold me near, you drown out the crowd.
Try as they may, they can never defy
What's been said between your heart and mine.

The smile on your face *etc.*

Wonderwall

Words & Music by Noel Gallagher

Vocals Level 1 - Male

Help!

Words & Music by
John Lennon & Paul McCartney

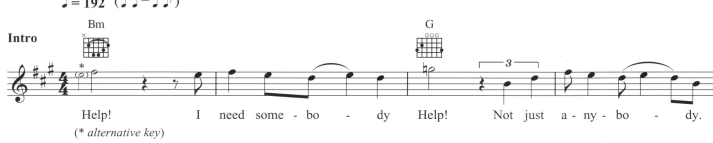

Help! I need some-bo-dy Help! Not just a-ny-bo-dy.

(* *alternative key*)

Help! You know I need some-one.___ Help!___

Verse

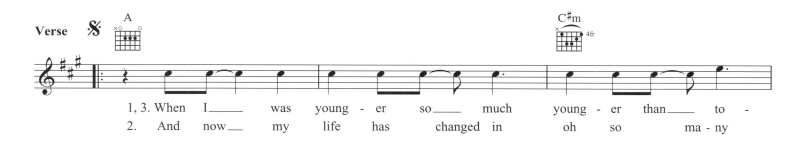

1, 3. When I___ was young-er so___ much young-er than___ to-
2. And now___ my life has changed in oh so ma-ny

-day,___ I nev-er need-ed a-ny bo-dy's
ways,___ my in-de-pen-dence seems___ to

help in a-ny way.___ But now these
va-nish in the haze.___ But ev-'ry

days are gone___ I'm not so self-as-sured,___
now and then___ I feel so in-se-cure,___

Unchained Melody

Words by Hy Zaret
Music by Alex North

Vocals Level 1 - Male

© Copyright 1954 (Renewed 1982) Frank Music Corporation, USA.
MPL Communications Limited.
All Rights Reserved. International Copyright Secured.

This music is copyright. Photocopying is illegal.

That'll Be The Day

Words & Music by Buddy Holly,
Norman Petty & Jerry Allison

Vocals Level 1 - Male

Your Song

Words & Music by
Elton John & Bernie Taupin

Vocals Level 1 - Male

Coda

I hope you don't mind,__ I hope you don't mind__ that I put down in__ words

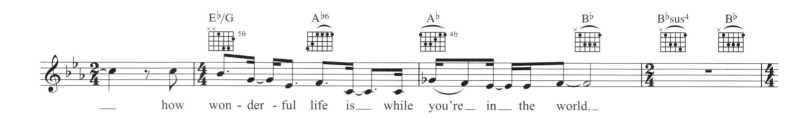

__ how won-der-ful life is__ while you're__ in__ the world.__

I hope you don't mind,__ I hope you don't mind__ that I put__ down in__ words__

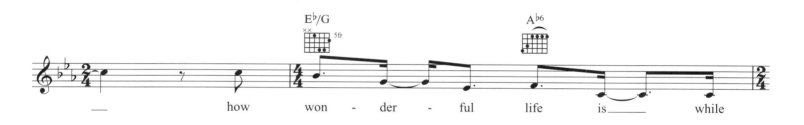

__ how won - der - ful life is__ while

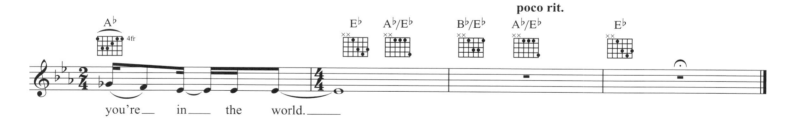

you're__ in__ the world.__

Verse 3:
I sat on the roof and kicked off the moss,
Well a few of the verses, well they've got me quite cross.
But the sun's been quite kind while I wrote this song,
It's for people like you, that keep it turned on.

Verse 4:
So excuse me forgetting but these things I do,
You see, I've forgotten if they're green or they're blue,
Anyway the thing is what I really mean,
Yours are the sweetest eyes I've ever seen.

And you can tell everybody, *etc.*

Grade 3 *Technical Exercises*

In this section, the examiner will ask you to perform the four exercises printed below. You do not need to memorise the exercises (and you may use the book in the exam) but the examiner will be looking for the speed and confidence of your response. The examiner will also give you credit for the level of your musicality.

Exercise 1: Rhythm

Disc 2 Track 3

You will be asked to perform the exercise below as written to a backing track accompaniment in the exam. A short sound check will be given.

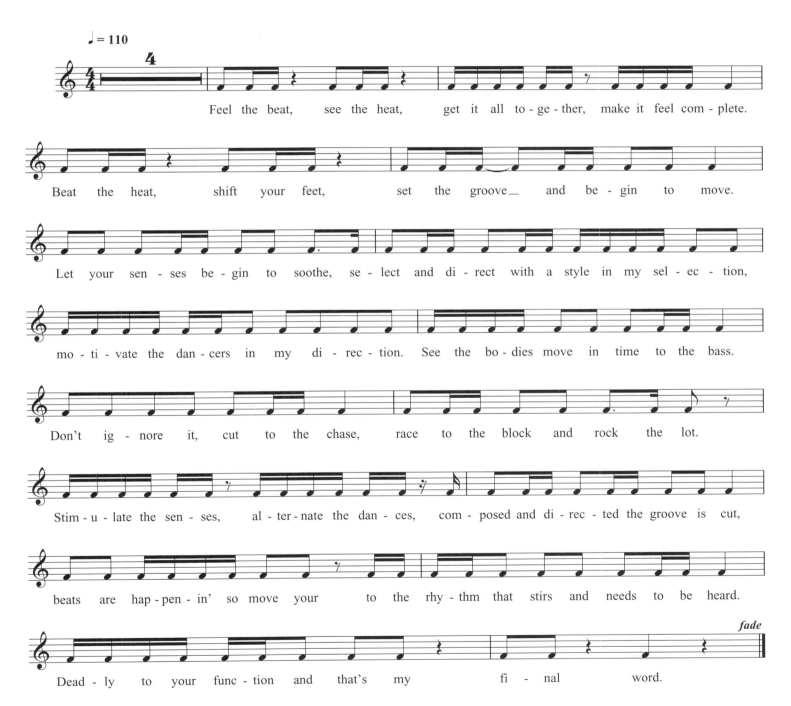

Vocals Level 1 - Male

37

You will be asked to perform a major, natural minor, harmonic minor and major pentatonic scale in the following rhythms. You will be allowed to choose your own starting note from **A-E** which will be played to you before you begin. You will be asked a selection by the examiner and you will perform the exercise *legato* to a sound of your own choosing.

Major

Natural Minor

Harmonic Minor

Major Pentatonic

Exercise 3: Intervals

This exercise has two parts. (A) You will be asked to pitch a major or minor third, perfect fourth and perfect fifth by step above notes **I**, **IV** and **V** of the chosen key of the above scale. The examiner will play the note for four beats on a CD and you will be asked to sing as indicated.

Disc 2 Track 5

(B) You will be asked to pitch a major or minor third to root by step on the same notes. The examiner will play the interval for four beats on a CD and you will be asked to sing as indicated.

Exercise 4: Phrasing & Dynamics

Disc 2 Track 7

You will be asked to prepare the following exercise. The examiner will play the backing on CD and you will be asked to sing the exercise, paying attention to the written phrasing and dynamics. You may perform the exercise using any sound that you consider appropriate.

Yellow

Words & Music by Guy Berryman, Jon Buckland,
Will Champion & Chris Martin

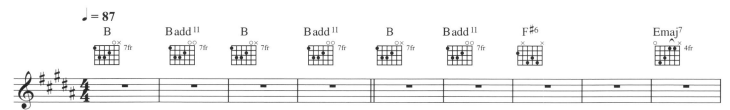

1. Look at the stars, look how they shine for____
(* alternative key)

____ you, and ev-'ry thing you__ do,____ yeah, they were all__ yel-low.__

(1.) I came a-long I wrote a song for____ you,
2. I swam a-cross I jumped a-cross for____ you,

and all the things you__ do,____ and it was called__ yel-low.__
oh, what a thing to__ do,____ 'cause you were all___ yel-low.__

I drew a line, So then I took my____ turn,
I drew a line for____ you,

oh, what a thing to've done,____ and it was all__ yel-low.
oh, what a thing to do,____ and it was all__ yel-low.

Vocals Level 1 - Male

(Sittin' On) The Dock Of The Bay

Words & Music by
Steve Cropper & Otis Redding

Disc 2 Track 10

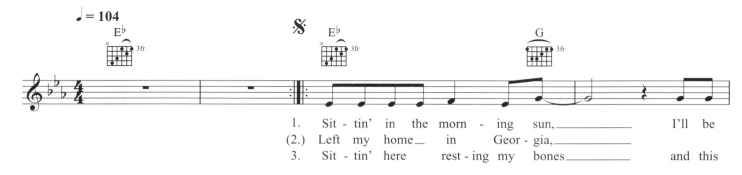

1. Sit-tin' in the morn-ing sun,_____ I'll be
(2.) Left my home_ in Geor-gia,_____ head-ed
3. Sit-tin' here rest-ing my bones_____ and this

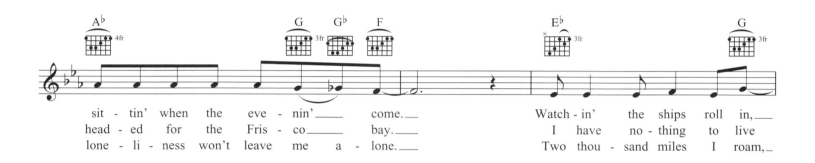

sit-tin' when the eve-nin'_____ come._ Watch-in' the ships roll in,_
head-ed for the Fris-co_____ bay._ I have no-thing to live
lone-li-ness won't leave me a-lone._ Two thou-sand miles I roam,_

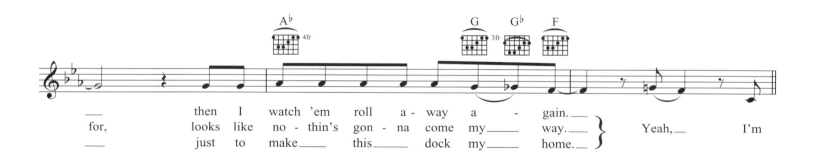

___ then I watch 'em roll a-way a-gain._ Yeah,_ I'm
for, looks like no-thin's gon-na come my_____ way._
___ just to make_____ this_____ dock my_____ home._

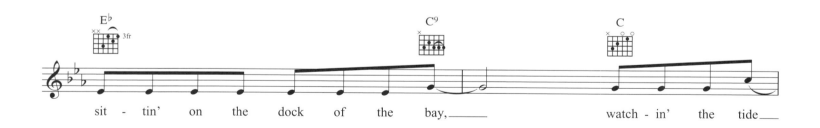

sit-tin' on the dock of the bay,_____ watch-in' the tide_

roll_ a-way._ Ooh,_ I'm just sit-tin' on the dock of the bay,_

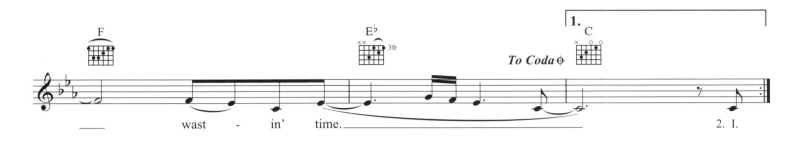

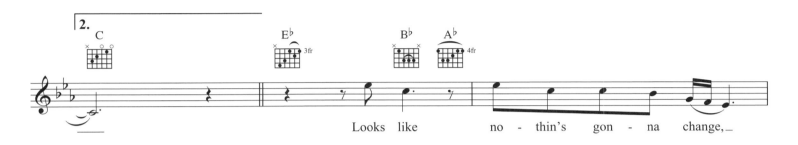

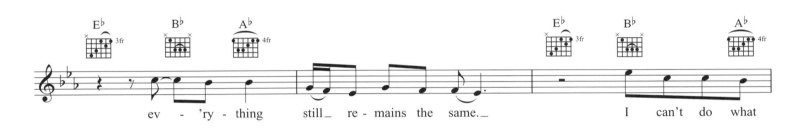

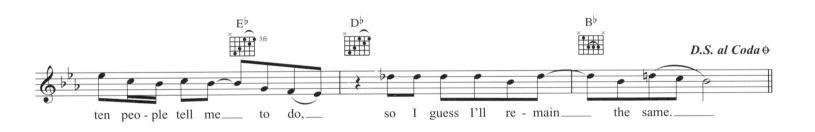

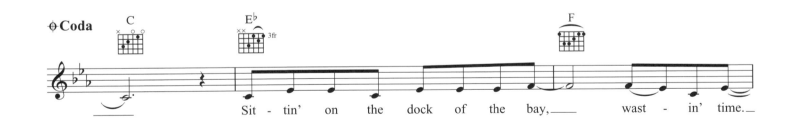

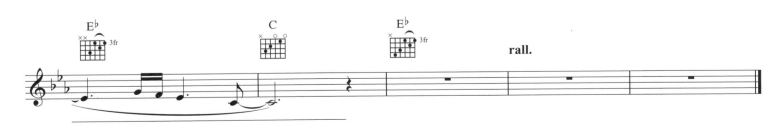

Blue Suede Shoes

Words & Music by Carl Lee Perkins

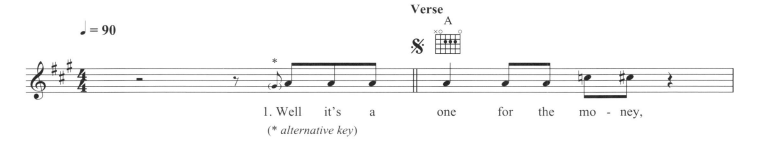

1. Well it's a one for the mo - ney,
(* alternative key)

two for the show, three to get-a read - y now go, cat, go. But don't

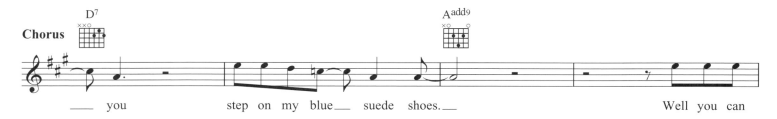

____ you step on my blue____ suede shoes.____ Well you can

do a - ny-thing____ but stay-ay off of my blue____ suede shoes._____ 2. Well, you can

knock me down,____ step on my face,____ sland - er my name____ all____
(3.) burn my house,____ steal my car,____ drink my li - quor from an

o - ver the place.____ } Well, do a - ny-thing____ that you wan - na do,____ but
old fruit jar.____ }

uh - uh ho - ney lay off____ of { them } shoes. And don't____ you
                                    { my }

Vocals Level 1 - Male

Roll With It

Words & Music by Noel Gallagher

Disc 2 Track 13/14

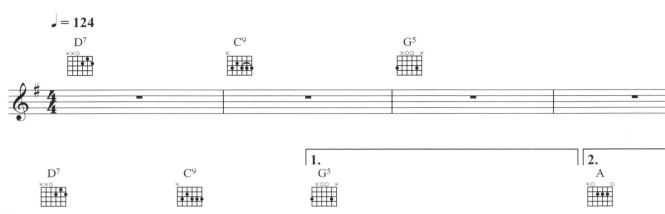

You got - ta roll___ with it, you got - ta take___ your time, you got - ta
(* *alternative key*)

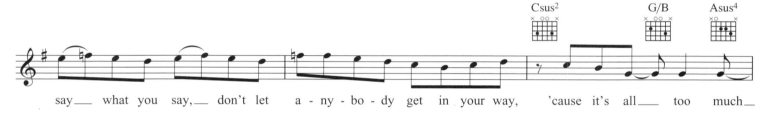

say___ what you say,___ don't let a - ny - bo - dy get in your way, 'cause it's all___ too much___

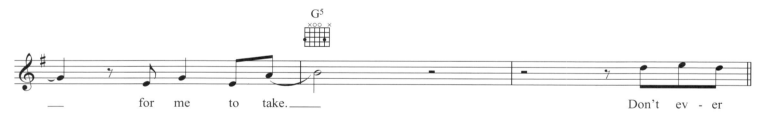

___ for me to take.___ Don't ev - er

stand___ a - side, don't ev - er be de - nied___ you wan - na be___ who you'd be___ if you're

com - in' with me.___ I think I've got a feel - in' I've lost___ in - side, I

Why Does It Always Rain On Me?

Words & Music by Fran Healy

Vocals Level 1 - Male

Rock DJ

Words & Music by Robbie Williams,
Guy Chambers, Kelvin Andrews,
Nelson Pigford & Ekundayo Paris

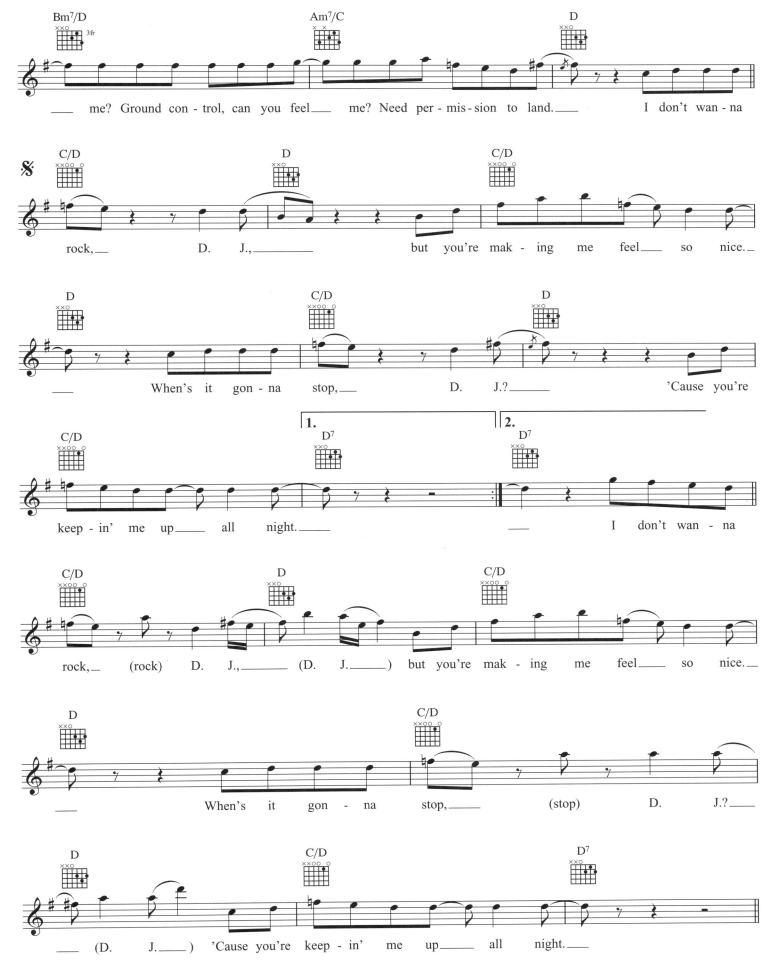

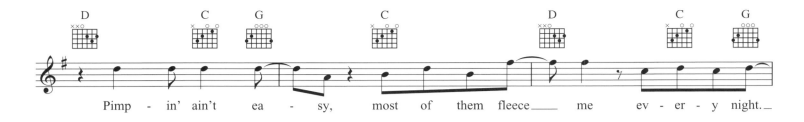

Pimp - in' ain't ea - sy, most of them fleece___ me ev - er - y night.___

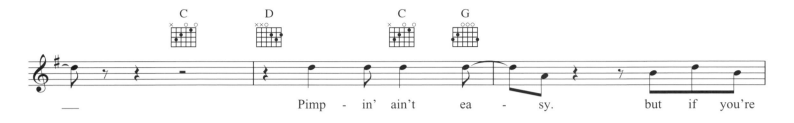

___ Pimp - in' ain't ea - sy. but if you're

sell - in' it,_____ it's al - right.____

D.S. (repeat chorus to fade)

Come on! I don't wan - na

Verse 2:

Singin' in the classes
Music for the masses
Give no head no backstage passes
Have a proper giggle
I'll be quite polite
But when I rock the mike, I rock the mike (right)
You got no love then you're with the wrong man
It's time to move your body
If you can't get a girl but your best friend can
It's time to move your body.

I don't wanna be sleazy
Baby, just tease me
Got no family planned
Houston, do you hear me?
Ground-control, can you feel me?
Need permission to land.

I don't wanna rock *etc.*

The Guru's Guide To Level 1 *Male Vocals*

Supplementary Material

Rockschool recommends the following songs in addition to the repertoire printed in this book. The list below shows the songs arranged by grade along with the publications in which they may be found.

Please note that the publications listed below are subject to change.

Grade 1

Heartbeat	*Play Guitar With Buddy Holly*	AM943734
Get Back	*Play Guitar With The Beatles*	NO90665
Town Called Malice	*Play Guitar With The Jam*	AM963391
Eight Days A Week	*Play Guitar With The Beatles Vol. 2*	NO90667

Grade 2

Yesterday	*Play Guitar With The Beatles*	NO90665
I Shot The Sheriff	*Play Guitar With Bob Marley*	EMF100617
Run To You	*Play Guitar With Bryan Adams - Early Years*	AM970475
Ticket To Ride	*Play Guitar With The Beatles Vol. 2*	NO90667
Right Here Waiting	*Essential Audition Songs: Pop Ballads*	IMP9776A
Lucy In The Sky With Diamonds	*Play Guitar With The Beatles Vol. 3*	NO90689
Don't Stand So Close To Me	*Play Guitar With The Police*	AM960993

Grade 3

Flying Without Wings	*Sing With Pop Idols*	AM974116
Here Comes The Sun	*Jam With The Beatles*	NO90685
You Wear It Well	*In Session With Rod Stewart*	IMP6607A
I Have A Dream	*Sing With The Boys*	AM969276
There She Goes	*Play Guitar With... Pop Anthems*	AM960982
Sit Down	*Play Guitar With... Pop Anthems*	AM960982
Lyin' Eyes	*Jam With The Eagles*	IMP4588A
Ain't No Sunshine	*Essential Audition Songs: Pop Ballads*	IMP9776A
50 Ways To Lose Your Lover	*Play Acoustic Guitar With Paul Simon*	PS11469
Life Is A Rollercoaster	*Stars In Your Eyes: Number 1 Hits*	IMP9028A
That'll Be The Day	*Play Guitar With Buddy Holly*	AM943734
Peggy Sue	*Play Guitar With Buddy Holly*	AM943734

Warm Up

It is important that you prepare for the exam by warming up your voice properly. You should ensure that you arrive at the exam centre within plenty of time to do this. We have arranged the elements of the grade exam so that the performances come at the end. The backing tracks and/or accompaniment are always variable in volume and you should always tell the examiner if you feel that you are straining to be heard.

Free Choice Pieces

In grade exams you are allowed to perform one song not specified in this book or the companion Level 1 *Female Vocals* book. This maybe a hit from the chart or a song composed by yourself. In performance certificate exams you are allowed to perform up to two songs not specified in this book.

If you wish to find out whether a free choice piece song is appropriate for the grade, you may either contact Rockschool and submit the song for adjudication, or look on our website www.rockschool.co.uk and consult the free choice piece criteria.

Marking Schemes

The table below shows the marking schemes for grade exams and performance certificates. All Rockschool exams are marked out of 100 and the pass mark for a grade exam is 65% and for a performance certificate is 70%.

Grade Exam

Element	Pass	Merit	Distinction
Technical Exercises	11 out of 15	12 out of 15	13 out of 15
General Musicianship Questions	3 out of 5	4 out of 5	5 out of 5
Aural Tests	6 out of 10	7 out of 10	8 out of 10
Piece 1 Piece 2· Piece 3	13 out of 20 13 out of 20 13 out of 20	15 out of 20 15 out of 20 15 out of 20	17 out of 20 17 out of 20 17 out of 20
Unaccompanied Piece	6 out of 10	7 out of 10	7 out of 10

Performance Certificate

Element	Pass	Merit	Distinction
Piece 1	14 out of 20	16 out of 20	18 out of 20
Piece 2	14 out of 20	16 out of 20	18 out of 20
Piece 3	14 out of 20	16 out of 20	18 out of 20
Piece 4	14 out of 20	16 out of 20	18 out of 20
Piece 5	14 out of 20	16 out of 20	18 out of 20

Examination Criteria

Rockschool examiners assess all examinations according to strict guidelines. Copies of these for vocals can be found on the website www.rockschool.co.uk or direct from our offices. Please ring 0845 460 4747 for further details.

Exam Regulations

Entering a Rockschool exam is easy. Please read through the instructions on the back of the entry form accompanying this book carefully, before filling it in. Information on current fees can be obtained by ringing Rockschool on 0845 460 4747 or by logging on to the website www.rockschool.co.uk.